The Living Book of the Living Theatre

with an introductory essay by Richard Schechner

New York Graphic Society Ltd.
Greenwich, Connecticut

Standard Book Number 8212-0233-2
Library of Congress Catalog Card Number 76-148667

Printed in Italy

THE LIVING THEATRE by Richard Schechner

Overhanging Rio de Janeiro are *favelas* — clusters of shacks stuck to the sides of steep hills. Views from these *favelas* are incredible — below is all of Rio and the sea, above are the mountains. Some *favelas* have more than 80,000 inhabitants, and these cities of the poor surround and threaten to fall in on Rio. The government only grudgingly acknowledges the *favelas,* providing them with minimal transport, electricity, water, sewerage, and police. But life is anything but chaotic. Once you climb to a *favela* you find everywhere webs of relationships made from family, community, crime, custom, and ceremony.

Were you to visit a *favela* during the summer of 1971 (December 1970 - March 1971) you would possibly hear people talking about a small group of Americans and Europeans doing simple, political plays, mostly without words, but seasoned with a few sentences of Portuguese. The *favelas* have no streets, so this is not street theater. They play in small courtyards, on the pathways, and where people gather to market. These players assemble, perform, disband, and reappear maybe five days later to ask people what they think of the play.

Thus Julian Beck and Judith Malina and some others of The Living Theatre — as up-to-date as I could find them. The Living itself was something of a mini-*favela* — a community of the poor sustained by any means necessary, kept out of the central cities, grudgingly acknowledged. Its moment of greatest public triumph — the American Tour of 1968-69 was also its moment of crack-up. But I want to be careful not to write premature epitaphs — for the Becks' great genius is for transformation.

The kernel of these changes are each other. His parents were middle-class New York Jews, and when he was a little boy his mother diligently took him to the Metropolitan, the Modern, the Frick, and down to Eva Le Gallienne's Civic Repertory Theatre on 14th Street. Her father was an orthodox rabbi who fled Kiel, Germany, in 1928 when Judith was two; her mother once had been an actress. In 1943 the son of the American distributor of Volkswagen parts met the daughter of the passionately anti-Nazi rabbi. He was 18, and she 17. They were interested in the same things — painting, politics, theater, each other — and they became fast friends. Julian tried Yale, but dropped out after less than a year. In the summer of 1944 he went to Provincetown and there met Paul Goodman. He saw the work of Pollock, Motherwell, Rothko, Kline, and de Kooning and realized that these artists were implying a life that the theater didn't know existed. In the fall of 1945 Judith won a partial scholarship to Erwin Piscator's Dramatic Workshop at the New School. Often she brought Julian to class with her as Piscator laid out the theories and practices of Epic Theatre.

Little by little, as is always the case, a destiny was mapped. It arose out of the avant-garde of the forties, and the shock of the War; it was fueled by Judith's burning wish to be an actress and Julian's more gentle genius for design and painting; it was given direction by Goodman and his understanding of philosophical and political anarchism; it was nourished by the life style of Greenwich Village and the free play it gave to a variety of sexual and social experiences.

Finally, in 1946, the Becks decided to make a theater of their own. Following the custom of the day, they sought the advice and support of famous people. A number of these complied, including Jean Cocteau, William Carlos Williams, Merce Cunningham, and Robert Edmond Jones. In 1947, Julian took his inheritance of $ 6,000 and with Judith formed The Living Theatre Productions, Inc. Their first manifesto said: « There is no final way of staging any play. (.....) And no play will be liked by all. We can only expect that our audience understand and enjoy our purpose, which is that of encouraging the modern poet to write for the theater ».

In 1948 they rented their first theater, a basement called the Wooster Stage. But they had hardly begun rehearsals for Ezra Pound's versions of some Noh plays when the police closed the theater, fearing it was a front for a whorehouse. Julian wrote Pound, and the poet replied: « How else cd a seeryus tee-ater suppot itself in N.Y.? ». In October, 1948, Julian and Judith married, and about nine months later their first child, Garrick, was born. From 1948 until 1951 the Living was at 789 West End Avenue — the Becks' apartment. On Thursday evenings the spacious living room was given over to talks, gatherings, readings, and, from time to time, a performance. In March 1951, a friend, Richard Gerson, asked the Becks to mount his play, *The Thirteenth God,* and gave them enough money for a two-week run at the Cherry Lane Theatre. Judith directed and played the female lead, and Julian made the sets and costumes.

A few months later, the Becks staged four one-acts in their West End Avenue apartment. These plays by Goodman, Stein, Brecht, and Lorca ran for three weeks. In July, 1951 — a month before the one-acts opened at home the Becks signed a one-year lease on the Cherry Lane. On December 2, 1951 they opened Stein's, *Dr. Faustus Lights the Lights.* William Carlos Williams wrote them: « I am walking in a dream, the aftermath of what I saw and heard at your Cherry Lane Theatre last evening. (.....) It is so far above the level of commercial theater that I tremble to think it may fade and disappear ». On March 2, 1952 they opened *An Evening of Bohemian Theatre* — plays by Stein, Picasso, and Eliot. The bill was an enormous success, running for fourteen weeks.

The fire department hassled the Becks and they did not renew their lease on the Cherry Lane. They looked for more than a year before renting a loft on West 100th Street. « With no money, with lumber scavenged from the debris of houses being torn down in the neighborhood, with a curtain made from the remnants of the costumes for *Ubu the King* and chairs gathered from all over the city, a theater was shaped and opened in March, 1954, with W. H. Auden's *The Age of Anxiety* ». Auden was followed by Strindberg and Cocteau, and then Pirandello's *Tonight We Improvise,* another huge success.

Let us condense in the interest of economy. The Becks were launched on a traditional avant-garde career. They touched all the bases and had won their right. They were the bright hope of a group who wanted to see the theater restored to poetry, sensibility, social consciousness, and art. They were destined (so their friends hoped) to carry into the theater the renewal of the arts which the New York School brought to painting, Cunningham to dance, Goodman to social thought, and Williams to poetry.

The first great transformation of the Becks was meeting each other and fusing his gentleness to her fire; the second was growing into the New York avant-garde. The third was their participation in the Peace Movement. They had long been theoretically interested in politics, but in 1955 through the connection of Jackson MacLow, the poet, Judith participated in a protest against compulsory air raid drills. She was among a small band of protesters who were arrested when they refused to depart to a shelter.

Increasingly over the years, as we all know, the Becks joined in and led non-violent, anarchistic actions against war, nuclear testing, and regulations and systems which they felt oppressive. Their first experience with street theater came not through theater at all, but through the actual pageantry of political awakening which swept America in the late fifties and sixties. They saw the inside of courts and spent time in jails. The separation between art and politics which was one of the standbys of traditional avant-gardism appeared at first foolish, later dangerous, and ultimately evil. The barriers between art and life were being battered down from all sides. If the police could storm into a theater and close it, why couldn't theater people close the police?

In 1955, after police and Buildings Department harrasment, the Loft was closed. It was not until June, 1957, that the Becks found the building on the corner of 6th Avenue and 14th Street that became their last theater in America — and their last permanent theater anywhere. They renovated, and on January 13, 1959, opened Williams' *Many Loves.* More important, during 1958 they read Artaud's *The Theatre and Its Double* and this book stimulated their aesthetic growth as jail did their political growth — radicalizing them and making them learn that the future of the theater was not in literature but in action.

The first play in which the Becks applied Artaudian principles was Jack Gelber's *The Connection* which opened at the 14th Street Theater on July 16, 1959. Gelber's play was out front with its strong language, its discussion of drugs, its use of the house and lobby as acting areas, its integration of music, its low-key but ruthless acting style. *The Connection* caused controversy and the Becks were suddenly famous. Their theater won a *Village Voice "Obie"* and they were invited to the Théâtre des Nations in Paris, where they won the Grand Prize.

As is often the case, success meant a gigantic leap in expenses and an inability to pay for what was now expected of them. While productions at the Cherry Lane had sometimes cost less than $ 100, maintaining 14th Street cost $ 3,300 per week. Steadily the Living sank into debt. As Julian said in 1962, « We're in the terrible position of being destroyed by our own success ».

Push came to shove during the run of Kenneth H. Brown's *The Brig,* a masterpiece of cruelty and precision. *The Brig* opened in May, 1963 — by fall the Living was so deep in debt that the landlord got a court order for eviction and the Internal Revenue Service sent agents in to occupy the theater on the night of October 18-19. Actors and friends were inside the building. The IRS men let anyone out who wanted to come out, but no one in. However, some audience sneaked in over adjoining roofs and down back walls to a contraband performance of *The Brig.*

I remember standing in 6th Avenue with a megaphone made from a picket sign shouting questions up to Judith who answered them into a microphone; she later threw the tape down to me for transcription. I asked her what would happen if the $ 50,000 necessary to keep the Living alive wasn't found. « We are prepared to embark on an entirely differently financed theater, a different kind of theater », she said. « What kind? », I asked. « A theater not so dependent on constant fund-raising. (.....) There is much interest in The Living Theatre in Europe. We have lots of plans ».

The 14th Street Theater was closed, the Becks were later tried for their tax debt and jailed for contempt of court, and the Living went to Europe — to those years of exile that transformed this experimental theater into an experiment in communal, nomadic living and collaborative creativity. It is here that the book in front of you catches up with the Living. For it is in Europe that the theater makes *Antigone* and *Mysteries, Frankenstein* and *Paradise Now.* Then in 1968 the Living comes back to America, not to stay but to tour. Everywhere the theater goes, it stirs a large following — in New Haven, New York, Los Angeles and dozens of other places. The tour over, the Living sails back to Europe in the spring of 1969. The following year the theater splits up into « cells », and I lose track of them except for Judith and Julian and a few others in Brazil. In the summer of 1970 I get a book of *21 Songs of the Revolution* — by Julian Beck.

« VII.

      not only do i ponder and find error and seek to alter the universe which oppresses me but i love it »

New York, January 1971

THE LIVING BOOK OF THE LIVING THEATRE

This is not a book about the Living Theatre, this is the Living Theatre. It is as much a presentation of the group as any theatrical spectacle. It is the essential philosophy of a group which overturned classic and experimental dramatic forms to replace them with political protest and moral anarchy. The Living Theatre's point-of-view is here expressed in words and photographs which alternate between daily life and the stage. Poetic and political statements alternate, rich images follow one another, sometimes lyric, sometimes tragic, but universal in their denunciation of the alienating structure of capitalist society.

The Living Theatre, founded by Judith Malina and Julian Beck, went beyond revolutionizing contemporary drama to represent a life-style of its own. In its years of activity, the group opened new worlds of political and social action to audiences in the United States and Europe. Because of this, it was constantly in conflict with those forces representing established values and patterns of behavior.

This book has no single author. It is the result of a group effort, including even those who, in the spirit of the Living Theatre, worked on the technical aspects of producing the physical book. It is a unique, revolutionary signpost, pointing toward possible new paths for the future.

Jenny Hecht
Henry Howard
Nona Howard
Ben Howard
Mary Mary
Leonardo Treviglio
Judith Malina
Julian Beck
Isha Manna
Steve Thompson
Rufus Collins
Sandy Linden
Cal Barber
Yessen Barber
Margie Barber
Diane Van Tosh
Erminio Bottura

Peter Weiss
Karen Weiss
David Van Tosh
Steve Ben Israel
Gunther Pannewitz
Tay Pannewitz
Roy Harris
Karl Einhorn
Jimmy Tyroff
Luke Theodor
Mal Clay
Jetty Clay
Gino Clay
Allan
Frank
Birgit Knabe
Odile Pannewitz

Pamela Badik
Petra Vogt
Pierre Biner
Rod Beer
Patty
Holy
Jimmy Anderson
Bill Shary
Dorothy Shary
Michael Shary
Gene Gordon
Michele Gordon
Carlo Silvestro
Silvia Fardella
Maurizio Del Borgo
Fabio Ciriachi
Giovanni Facetti
Paul Lawson

a is for alice

n is for new

a is for another or also

r is for reefers rebirth and repose

c is for cock c is for cunt

h is for harvest

y is for you

I'll tell you
what we need is more raving brothers and sisters so put these words down jump out of place smoke dope drop pills get laid run hysterical in the streets stick your hand right up that ladies dress and dig her big fat sticky thigh with the juices flowing barriers being broken and...
Can we be human
who A. stand B. sit (choose one) immaculately by while entire existence is being created and destroyed and created again with each moment. To grab on to an instant in such a way that we cannot respond brutalized and systematically to the new event current imagination is serving up to sicken even the strongest...
Dreams of power and control and systems of government
all equally and collectively guilty for the destruction of Alexandria and Hiroshima as well as for the creation of the everlasting dark ages in order to purposely perpetuate a system under which we have become a race that can neither plant the earth nor reap the harvest without causing harm and so have invented theories to explain, to make clear... the killing of an entire race, the Indian
Gone...
So that we as king can rule
Where once man and woman lived.
Six million Jews how many Vietnamese every worker who ever for profit and Bolivia and Biafra and Birmingham and here we go again. Oh America Oh Russia Oh China where are you going. Oh England France and Germany what possible goal can you have for a plan that has driven a civilization mad. Why?
Yet everywhere
Individuals are getting together to exchange information and find out where each other is at so that physical plans can be made by collectives of people interested in affecting the type of conscious necessary to replace movie images with human beings, profit with joy, guns with cocks and negative and destructive style of life with a positive and active celebration of being.
In the Spring of 1967, a commune was started in California by young people interested in building an alternative to present Mammon society without violence and with the production of the food and the supplies necessary to provide for its own needs and desires. It was one of many already in existence.
In the Summer of 1967, the Diggers opened a free store to add to the free food, free housing and free media program already existing in the Haight Ashbury community.
In 1968, agents of the state closed the Tolstoy Farm in Oregon.
In 1968, the first communes in Norway were started.
There are over 3,000 such gatherings of people giving birth of themselves in paradise now.
In the Summer of 1968, one group in Chicago and another in France manifested themselves within the framework of the old society in such a way as to insure that Hubert Humphrey would not be elected President of the United States and to cause the ultimate downfall of Charles De Gaulle in France. It is part of the growing demand for an immediate end to all forms of repression.
In March of 1969, near Alamagordo, New Mexico, on the date the first atomic death device was tested, a group of visionaries met to discuss, exhibit, and instruct in the creation of the technology necessary to run the new world without bureaucracy and without the profit motive.

In August 1969, after five days of fighting and 150 injuries, a group of striking Turkish workers were given a deadline by police to surrender an occupied factory. Five minutes before the deadline the workers threw open the doors, ran out, lifted the police on their shoulders and began to sing and dance.

Over 1,000,000,000 other beautiful people are searching for ways to create the forms capable of ending violence and feeding all the people so that man can begin to establish himself in a larger relation to the universe.

Every day more and more people stop and take a moment out. They look... touch... kiss... and then go on. This is the beginning of the total anarchy. Learn to breathe again. Learn to feel again. Learn to live again.

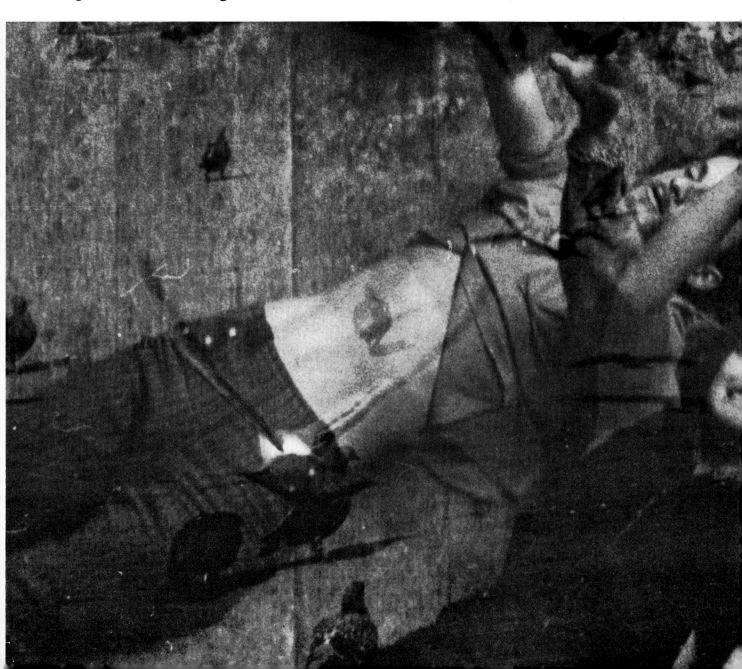

THE TRIP

At the full moon in July we arrived in Paris and went to an Arab café...

At the full moon in August one of us went mad in London, and Steve was hit by a truck while marching in the streets...

At the full moon in September we gathered in a cellar in London and spoke for the first time of Frankenstein...

At the full moon in October we were rehearsing the Mysteries in Paris.

At the full moon in November we played the Brig in Berlin for millions on television...

At the full moon in December I was in jail in New Jersey...

At the full moon in January I visited Julian in jail in Connecticut...

At the full moon in February we played the Mysteries in the Carre circus in Amsterdam...

At the full moon in March we played the Brig in Turin...

At the full moon in April we played the Mysteries in Rome...

At the full moon in May we performed the Brig in Naples...

At the full moon in June Garry was sick in Paris...

At the full moon in July we had a Chinese dinner with Elsa Morante in Berlin...

At the full moon in August we completed the structure for Frankenstein in Berlin...

At the full moon in September we were rehearsing Frankenstein desperately in Berlin...

At the full moon in October we returned from Venice to Berlin...

At the full moon in November we played the Maids and the Mysteries at the Intercontinental in Frankfurt...

At the full moon in December we travelled from Malmö to Göteborg.

At the full moon in January we arrived in Bologna...

At the full moon in February we played the Mysteries at the Palazzo Durini in Milan twice in a day...

At the full moon in March we travelled from Catania to Siracusa where we saw the Greek Theatre by moonlight...

At the full moon in April we celebrated the Seder in a hotel room in Banja Luka Yugoslavia after performing the Mysteries...

At the full moon in May we played the Brig in Parma...

At the full moon in June we were rehearsing Frankenstein in Reggio Emilia...

At the full moon in July we were returning from the Theatre of Nations in Paris, over the Alps, back to Italy...

At the full moon in August we opened Frankenstein in Cassis in a new production at the sea's edge...

At the full moon in September we played Frankenstein in Berlin...

At the full moon in October we played the Mysteries in Venice and staged the Lachmyian juggernauts for Antigone...

At the full moon in November we played the Mysteries in Amsterdam and rehearsed the entrance of Antigone with Polyneikes...

At the full moon in December we played the Mysteries in Amsterdam and rehearsed the faces of the people for Antigone...

At the full moon in January we staged the prologue for Antigone in Krefeld...

At the full moon in February we played Antigone in Dinslaken...

At the full moon in March we rehearsed the Bacchus Dances in Perugia in the freezing Palazzo...

At the full moon in April Julian flew to Morocco, and we played the Maids at the Palazzo Durini in Milan...

At the full moon in May we played Frankenstein in Naples...

At the full moon in June most of the company travelled to Rome to make a movie...

At the full moon in July I was in the American hospital in Paris with Isha Manna two days old...

At the full moon in August we walked with Garry in the Latin Quarter and visited the Orangerie in Paris where we were rehearsing Frankenstein...

At the full moon in September we performed the Mysteries in Paris and moved from Isha's birthplace on the Rue Troyon...

At the full moon in October we performed Antigone in Brussels...

At the full moon in November we performed Bussotti's opera « Passion according to de Sade » and quelled a rio on stage with a sit-in in Bordeaux...

At the full moon in January we performed Antigone in Lucerne and rehearsed a new staging of the messeng scene...

At the full moon in February we were settling into Cefalú, Sicily, preparing to rehearse Paradise Now...

At the full moon in March we were rehearsing Paradise Now in Cefalú and Julian made a lecture on John Cage

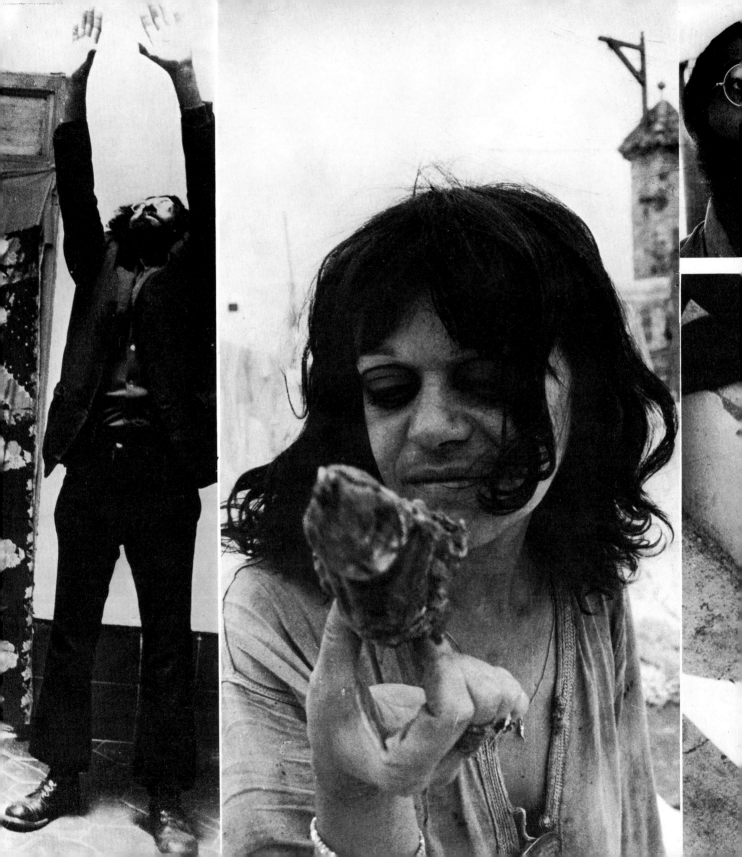

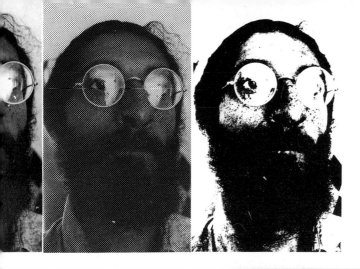

the full moon in April we celebrated the Seder in Cefalú and rehearsed the Totem Poles for Paradise Now...

the full moon in May we visited cathedrals of Tours and Chartres and arrived in Paris at midnight at the start of the General Strike...

the full moon in June we worked on the staging of the Rites for Paradise in the Garden of the Palace of the Popes in Avignon...

the full moon in July we held our first rehearsal on the stage of the Cloister of the Carmelites...

the full moon in August we worked on the Actions for Paradise in the Garden of Voltaire's house in Geneva...

the full moon in September we were on the M.S. Aurelia en route for an American tour holding a meeting on conscientious objectors...

the full moon in October we played Frankenstein in Brooklyn...

E CAMPIO FORTIS

At the full moon in **November we played Paradise Now at the Massachusetts Institute of Technology for which we were banned, and attended an anti-election rally on Boston Common...**

At the full moon in **December we played the Mysteries at Denison University in Granville, Ohio...**

At the full moon in **January we played the Mysteries at Hunter College in New York City...**

At the full moon in **February we played the Mysteries at Hays State College in Hays, Kansas...**

At the full moon in **March we arrived in San Francisco, moved into Ferlinghetti's office and took part in the occupation of the Straight Theatre...**

At the full moon in **April we celebrated the Seder in mid-Atlantic on the M.S. Europa...**

At the full moon in **May we were in Grenoble worrying about a warrant for offending morals brought against Mysteries from Besançon...**

At the full moon in **May we played Paradise in St. Etienne on Julian's 44th birthday...**

At the full moon in **June we travelled from London to Paris en route to Morocco...**

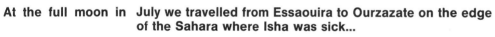

At the full moon in   July we travelled from Essaouira to Ourzazate on the edge of the Sahara where Isha was sick...

At the full moon in   August we were in Essaouira finishing the text of Paradise, beginning the text of Mysteries...

At the full moon in   September we were in Taormina rehearsing Antigone in the Teatro Antico and planning the new work...

At the full moon in   October I was in Paris for lunch with Jean-Jacques Lebel and took the night train to Milan where the company played Mysteries in the circus...

At the full moon in   November I was in Rome waiting for Carl to arrive while the company played Mysteries in Urbino...

At the full moon in December we played Paradise in Brussels...

At the full moon in January we had an Action Cell meeting in Pierre Clementi's house in Croissy planning new work...

At the full moon in February we had an Action Cell meeting in Pierre Clementi's house in Croissy planning new work and debated the ideologies of revolution and violence...

MYSTERIES &SMALLER PIECES

Jai Jai Jai Jai Sri Rama Ki Jai
Rama Bhagata Hanuman Ki Ja
Jai Shiva Shankar Kailash Pat
Jai Jai Gauri Ma Parvati,
Raghu Pati Raghaw Raja Ram
Sri Krishna Govinde Hare
Murare,
He Nath Narain Vasudeva.
Om Buddha, Om Mane Padme
Hum,
Om Brahma Vishnu Sadasiva.
Sarada Devi Ki Jai Ho,
Om Namo

I believe, that earth is in a continuous Cycle of Evolution and has to be.
I believe, that man has to change, in order to evolute.
I believe, that openness towards change and experience are essential for Life.
I believe, that defences within a human being are natural, in order to make us realize that we have change.
I believe, that differentiation in realities and behavior are important, so that we may learn from each oth to know what our position and value on this planet in this single and unique life is.
I believe, that we are all messengers towards each other, to help each other to realize our dreams.
I believe, that we have to love one another or die.
I believe, that love is the result of understanding based on experience.
I believe, that I love you, but give me a chance.
I believe, that I am, what I am and I become what I do.
I believe, that every human being is good but we have to give each other the chance to be according our own needs and desires.
I believe, that man is a servant to God, so we are servants towards each other because we are created his image.
I believe, that we have a basic desire to help each other and our life's hope is to reach the fullest exte of our individual power and value in which money is of less importance.
I believe, that honesty, imagination and the belief in ourselves are basic towards a better universe.
I believe, that rigidity is death.

I believe, that there is no death but life.
I believe, that pain is as valuable as pleasure.
I believe, that we have to signal towards each other, to tell each other where we are at, in order to make the destination clear in the chaos of this world.
I believe, that chaos and conflict are the beginning of creation.
I believe, that man starts to act self destructive towards himself and his fellow man once he stops experiencing himself.
I believe that experience is the ultimate answer towards a richer and fuller Life of understanding.
I believe, that the world is coming towards a Renaissance of true Life, in which art is no more artificial but Life itself, in which the ritual of daily Life becomes meaningful, in which the impossible becomes possible, where imagination and creation take power.
I believe in the big universal family and that we shall solve our problems.
God help us.
Love of Heart and mind.

à bas l'état   vive l'anarchisme

à bas la police   r   vive la liberté

à bas la violence   é   vive l'amour

à bas l'argent   v   vive le nouveau monde

à bas le capitalisme   o   vive l'humanité

à bas l'armée   l   vive la foi

à bas les prisons   u   vive l'individu

à bas la répression   t   vive la paix

à bas la guerre   i   vive la terre

à bas les frontières   o   vive l'unité

à bas les classes   n   vive la communauté

à bas l'avidité   vive la vérité

à bas le racisme

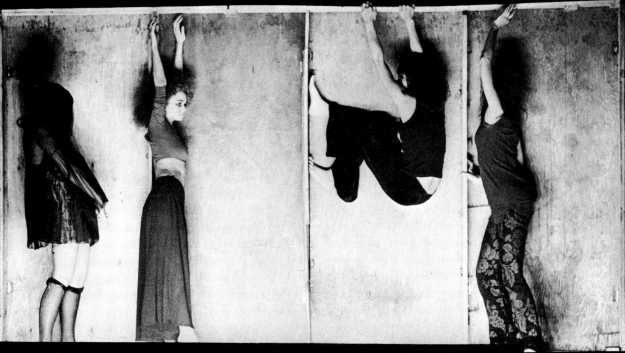

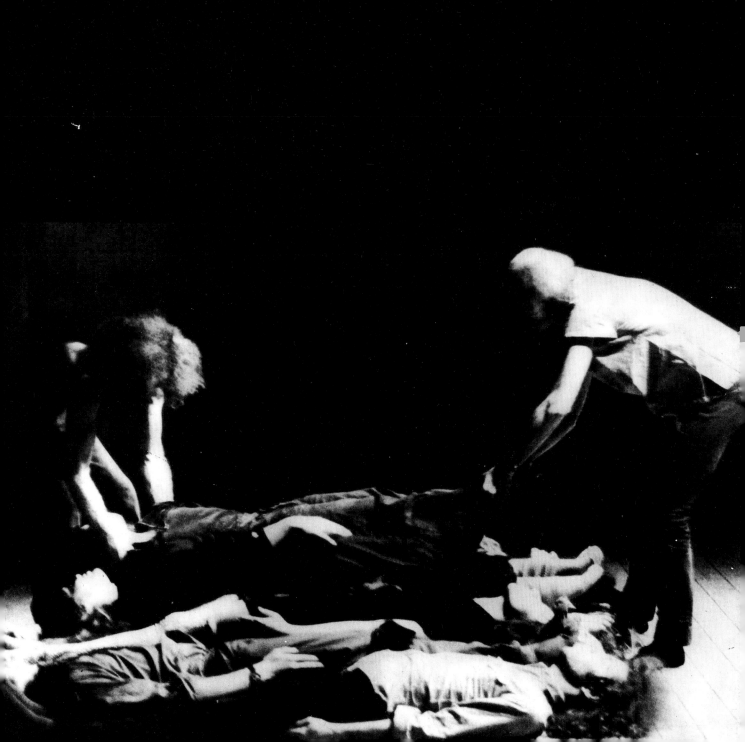

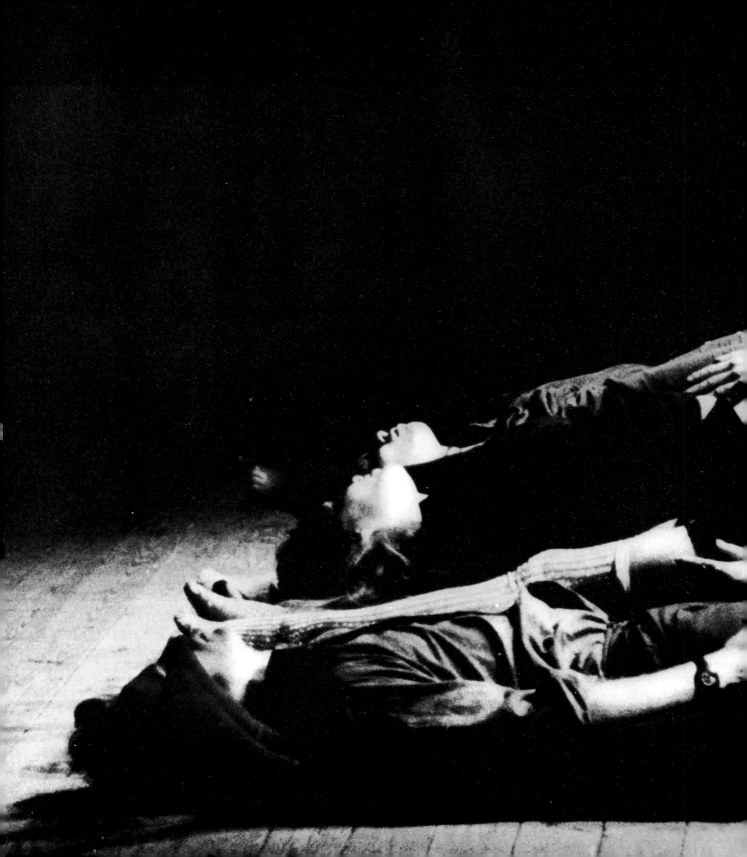

A WAY
OF
LIFE

being free is only a partial state of being

freedom is only the beginning

all creative action forms out of some kind of freedom

nothing bearable happens without some kind of freedom

after we get it there's beautiful work to do

nobody ever all free yet
i contest the suicide theory

all we want now is freedom
paradise one is the man woman freedom bird

paradise one walks freely

paradise two feels free
paradise two is free to worry about other things

to be free is to be free of hunger
to be free is to be free of privilege and the will of law
the external law of the state for instance

paradise three worries about things we can't worry about yet

paradise now is how to get there

paradise four is how to be and how not to be

there is only partial being with and without freedom

in paradise you are free
paradise is not everything

then come paradise five and then six and then maybe paradise
    sixty

it is because we know these things that we revolutionists
    bear the name of realists

Can I touch your soul
Yes I have known God in my madness
I am crying for life
Oh drop your gun
Stop smothering me
Let me breathe again the air
Give me back my sea my earth Rape
Her thighs are torn and bleeding
This mother with her last breath moans
Mind perception conception confusion
illusion destruction

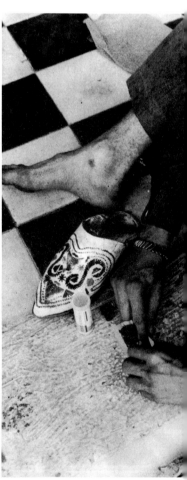

Let the starving dance again
the dances of harvest and feast
Let our numb bodies feel again without fear
I have a vision
I see us flying out of the abyss
I see us exploring and playing
in the universe
I am crying for life
Can I touch your soul.

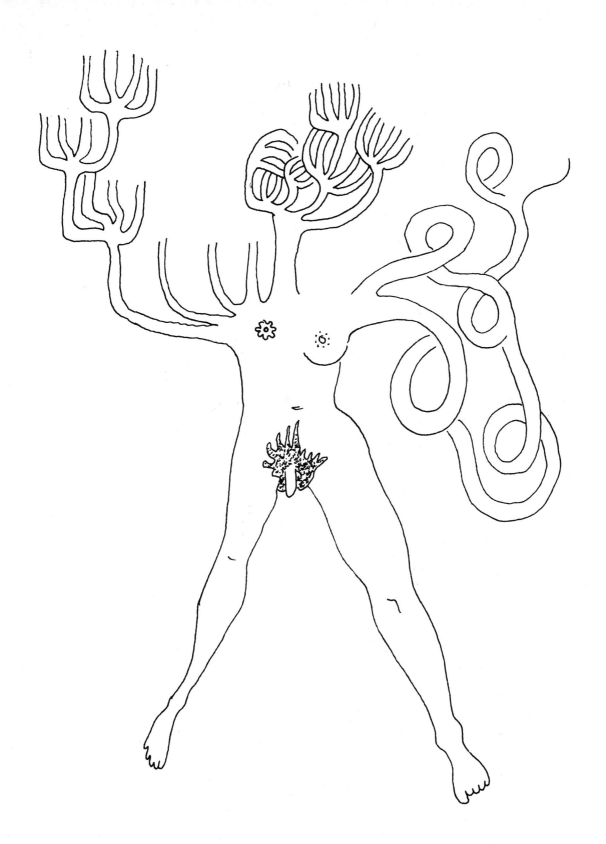

1. You always have the constitutional right to consult your attorney.
Insist on this right whenever you feel it is necessary.
2. **Prior** to arrest, you are **never** required to answer any police questions, except
a) name.
b) address.
c) where you are going.
and the policeman must have a good and lawful reason for asking even these questions.
3. **Nobody** has the right to search your home or your person
(or your hotel room, tent, locker, suitcase, purse, car, etc.) unless
a) you give him permission, or
b) he has a search warrant, or
c) you have been lawfully placed under arrest **before** the search.
Never let a policeman inside your door without a warrant unless you **want** him inside.
NEVER FORCIBLY RESIST ARREST.
4. If arrested, give no information except name, address, age, birthplace, etc.
Never discuss the facts of the charge against you; when questioned, refuse to answer, demand access
to a telephone and call your attorney. Remember, anything
you say can and will be used against you, despite any promise the police may make to you.
5. A policeman may stop a car at any time and demand to see a license to drive and the auto registration.
He may **not** arbitrarily search the car.
6. If you are arrested, call Bob Projansky at 212-228-3208 day or night and give your name, your
local address,
the charge against you, where you are being held and the telephone number.
Mention the Living Theatre and the answering service will accept the charges.

Dated: September 10, 1968

JERALD ORDOVER
One Liberty Street
New York, New York
HAnover 5-7520

A DECLARATION
PEACE AND FRIENDSHIP FOR ALL
LIFE ON EARTH AND THE UNIVERSE
A DRAFT

An end to all capitalist and exploitive imposition and law —
the class system x x x. The break down of the economic
structure of the bourgeois state by proving that it does not
exist once the worker-farmers non-violent revolution has
overthrown it. A workers-farmers-scientific-creative-social-
collective to be the voice, structure, genius of the revolutionary.
An end to all forms of violence through training and education.
The unconditional withdrawal of all armed and police forces
from foreign soil, underwater and space.
Disarming and destruction of all nuclear, germ, biochemical
and conventional weapons. Prohibition on war.
Cancelling of all contracts with corporate monopoly capital.
Collectivization of the means of production.
Collectivization of hospital and medical care.
Collectivization of natural resources.
Collectivization and establishment of natural health nurseries
and resorts for the new born, parents and children of all ages.
Building of the most modern housing collectives, urban,
suburban, country and farm by workers and farmers no longer
working for bourgeois monopoly capital but for themselves.
Establishment of collective communities.
Centralization of industry. All real estate and landed corporate,
theological and private institutional property to become that
of workers and farmers.
The end of the manufacture and growth of all produce
destructive to the health and well being of all life.
End of all forms of economic aid to foreign countries.
The settling of all economic debts with foreign countries —
end to economic trade.
The fullest self determination for males and females —
the popular vote.
Cutting of the number of hours and days to the work week in
accordance with the progression of change from a monopoly
capitalist state to a workers-farmers revolutionary collective.
Propelled by fuels of the collective genius, employment of the
most modern techniques for science, industry and
argriculture etc. through automation, so as to insure time
for the people to scientifically create new worlds of thought,
organically cleanse their bodies, be with their families
and loved ones.
The development and immediate production of electric and
or steam driven auto vehicles etc. Cleaning and revitalizing of
polluted earth, water and air.
Changing the diet. An end to the production of all
unnatural foods, etc. These to be taken out of the stores
and destroyed for being contaminated.
To be replaced by the collective farming of only organic
natural foods. End to the use of animals, reptiles and etc.
as « beasts of burden » and domestication. An educational
collective that represents the needs, wants, desires of the
collective community.
End to conscription. The releasing of all men and women
from the armed services. End to all law enforcement and
protection agencies.
End to the slaughter of animals, reptiles and etc. for the
purpose of eating and processing their flesh.
The construction of roads, highways, electric monorails,
railroad and airports. The opening of and end to all penal
institutions and releasing all those subjected to its
decadent institutional life.
All foods, housing, clothing and produce necessary for the
health and maintenance of the workers-farmers-scientific-
creative-social-collective to be that which comes out of the
collective life and shall be for those within it, free from
monetary or barter exchange. Dismemberment of the bank
and banning of its use as an institution and instrument
of exchange.
End to the use of gold etc. certificates and all means used
by bourgeois monopoly capitalism as a source of exchange

for commodities and labor power.

An end to barter and all means of exchange for life's birth right. The work done by the worker-farmers collective will be the combined strength of the collective.

Development of health centers, athletic fields, natural parks, etc. to further the organic and electromagnetic well being of all living beings.

An end to private and small business established under the system of bourgeois capitalism. Revitalization through use of the best forms of natural health care to prolong longevity.

Collectivization and establishment of new studies into preventive medicine through organically healthy bodies by way of diet, exercise and creative science.

The study and building of new cultural outlets for the expression of the workers-farmers-scientific-creative-social-collective.

The fullest and most expansive creative scientific research and exploration into universal space and earth, for the thorough health and maintenance of all life.

An end to mysticism, superstition and institutions that uphold those beliefs through theology and corrupt social systems.

The fullest expression of sexual freedom within a world where male and female plant and grow the seed to give birth to life.

The building of a world united front of workers-farmers revolutionaries and revolutionary collectives.

An end to all counter-revolutionary forces through the practice employment and fulfillment of the workers-farmers collective draft program.

Drawing of a constitution.

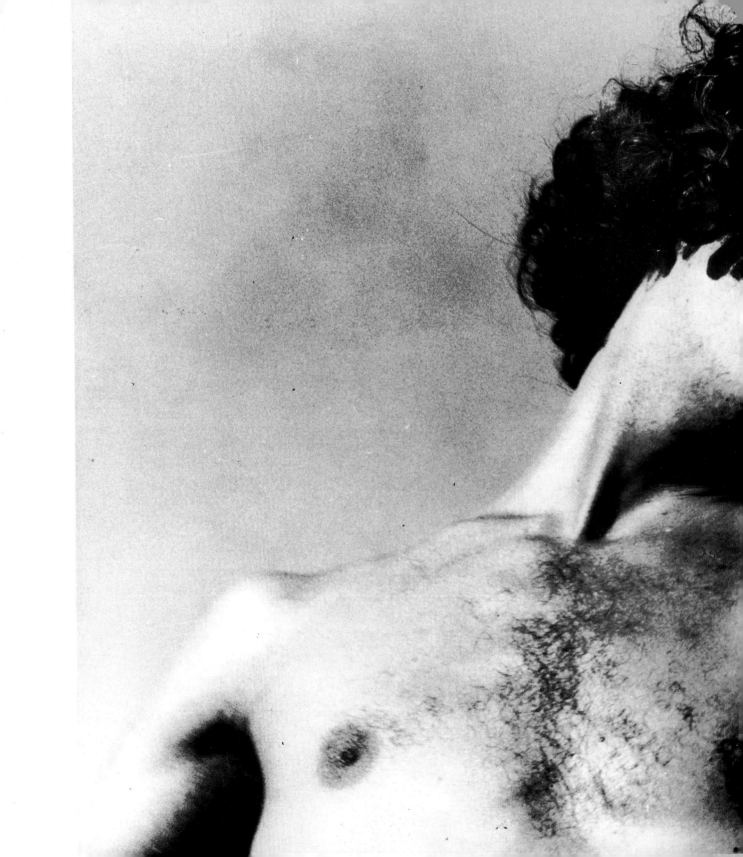

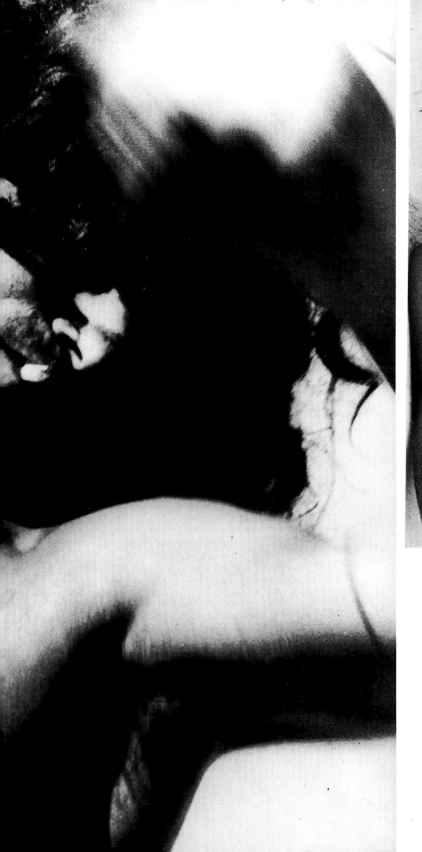

ODILE

JASON

PATTY

MALINA

EGO   SENSATION
IS   IS
THE   THE
GUIDE   GUIDE
TO   TO

LIBERATION

intuition.

BEHAVIOR   EXPERIENCE

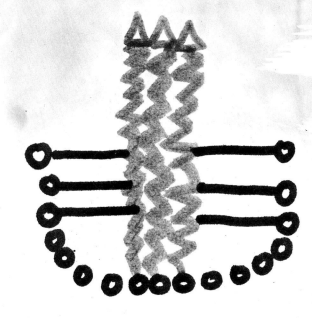

CEB

To L.T. My family
Thinking of you more than i could imagine / tales of julian in or at the Conferenza di stronzi in new york / oldest protestant church / flashes of steve wiping his arm pits with some magazine / that blonde cunt standing in front of me wagging her head in derision / days of glory / you must not put yourselves down so hard / enjoy our progress in enjoyment and reflection / you will see what your next step is / racked as always with the ability to see failures in our training / to aid the revolution selection of positive effective-ness / use it blow it up raise it / reaching for the unturned stone / to set the way right / find a theatrical experience which will blow it up / train to the spanish trains are nice / julian among your many activities try and drop me a line / judith one of your finely written post cards / counting on seeing carl in london / how to explain being with you has / given the ability to make some thing out of thin.

FRANKENSTEIN

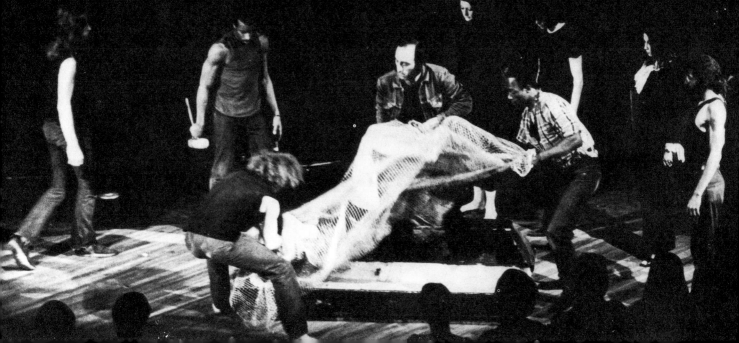

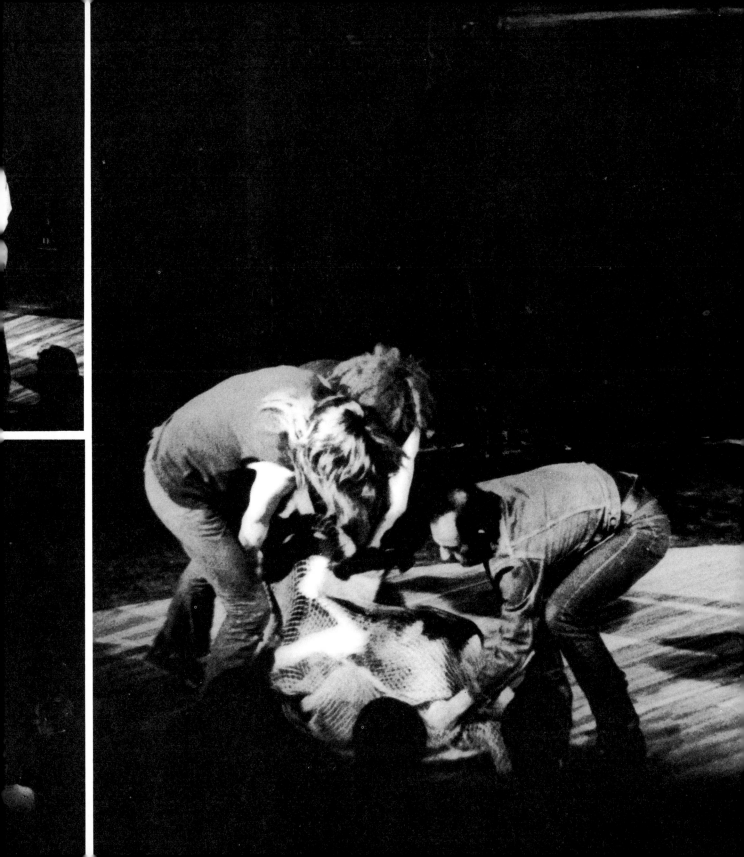

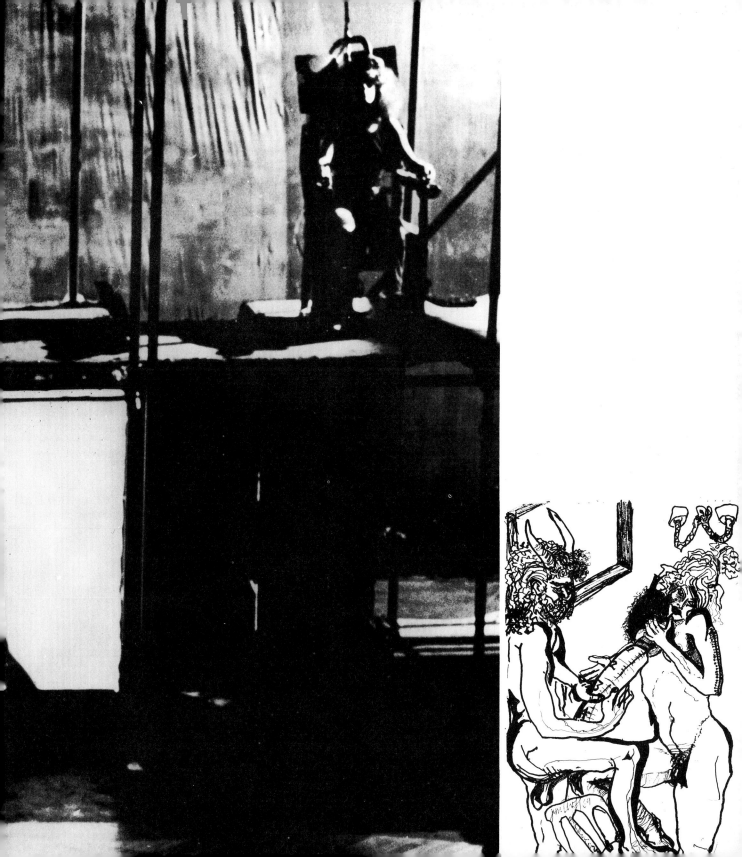

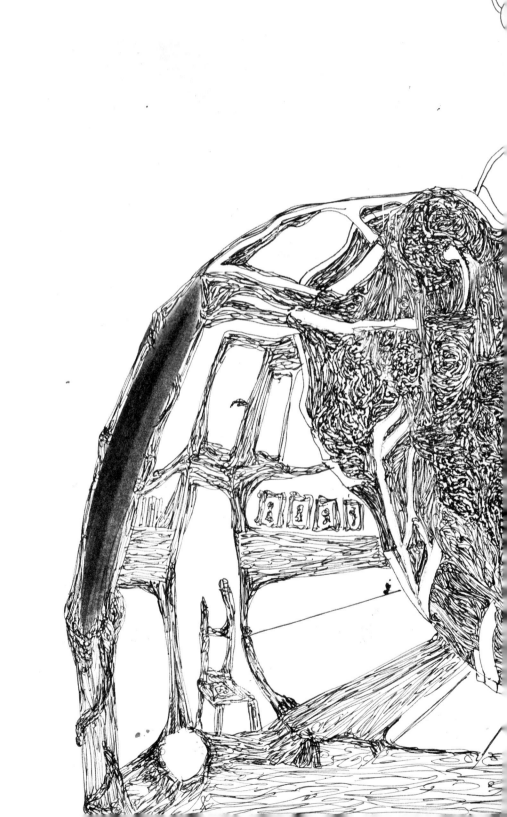

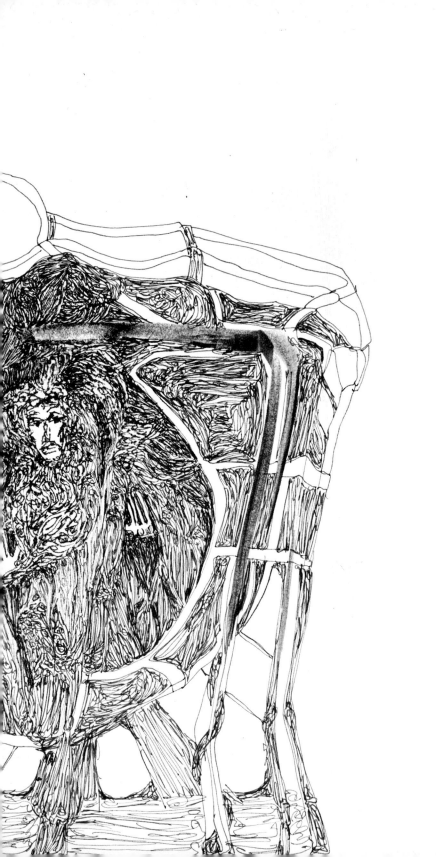

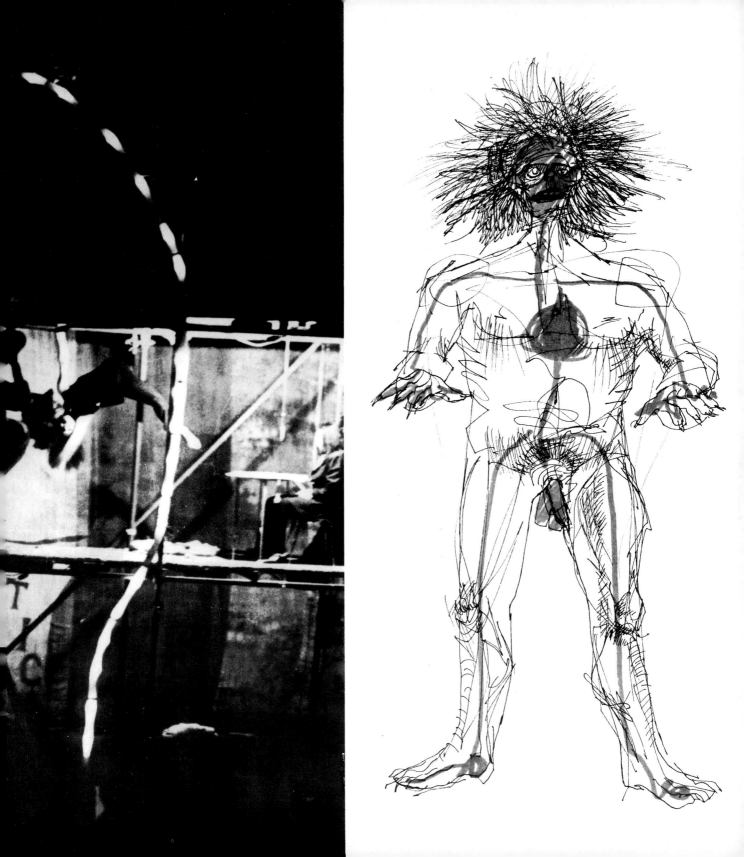

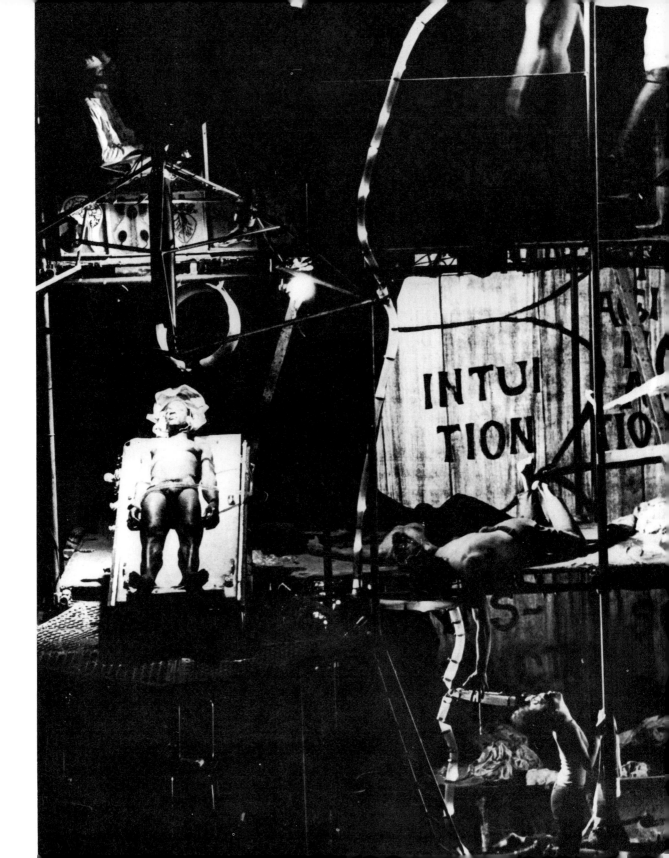

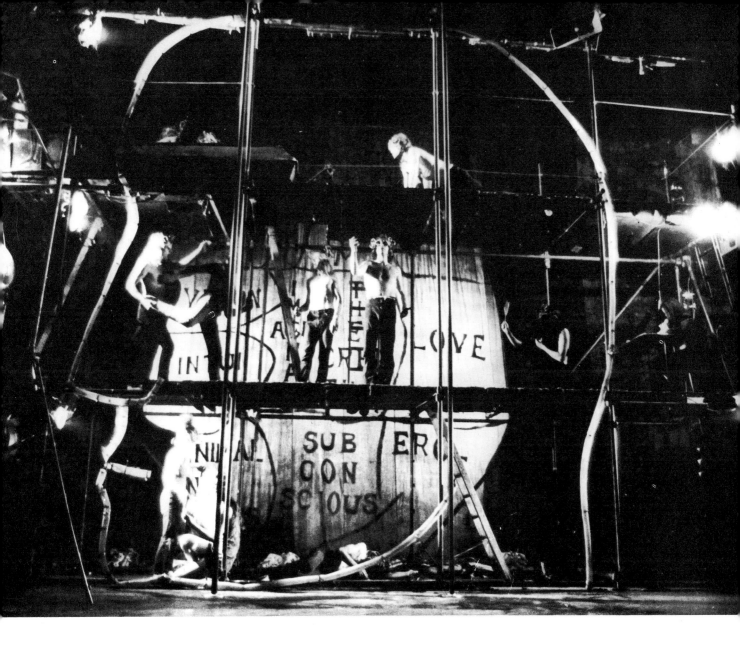

The Living Theatre has decided to withdraw from the Festival d'Avignon

1. Because, without using the word interdiction, all further performances of Paradise Now have been forbidden by the city in collaboration with the Administration of the Festival, under threat of repressive action and legal proceedings;

2. Because the patron of the Festival, the Mayor of Avignon, in collaboration with the Administration of the Festival, has forbidden all free performances in the streets of Avignon, although all tickets for the Festival have been sold, state categorically that they do not believe that the people are entitled to the theatre unless they can pay for it;

3. Because we have a choice between being dictated to by a Municipality and Festival Administration which wish under pretext to suppress our free expression as artists and between working for our own liberty and that of other people;

4. Because we have a choice between bowing down to a command disguised as a request, between accepting broken contractual terms, or withdrawing from a Festival which wishes to stop us from playing what we are contracted to play;

5. Because we wish to choose the solution which will lessen the violence in this city;

6. Because you cannot serve God and Mammon at the same time, you cannot serve the people and the state at the same time, you cannot serve liberty and authority at the same time, you cannot tell the truth and lie at the same time, you cannot play Antigone (which is about a girl who refuses to obey the arbitrary dictates of the state and performs a holy act instead) and at the same time substitute Antigone in the place of a forbidden play;

7. Because the time has come for us at last to begin to refuse to serve those who do not want the knowledge and power of art to belong to any but those who can pay for it, who wish to keep the people in the dark, work for the Power Elite, who wish to control the life of the artist and the lives of the people;

8. Because the time has come to liberate art and to remove its support from the Age of Humiliation and Exploitation.

9. Because the time has come to say No before our last shreds of honor are lost;

10. Because our art cannot be used any longer to represent authorities whose actions oppose what we believe in;

11. Because, altho it does not please us to lean on the justice of the law, we are convinced that our legal rights have been imposed on and broken, and that therefore we have been freed by this rupture to take this necessary action.

The company of the Living Theatre
Avignon 28 July 1968

ON TRAVAILLE ENSEMBLE POUR MANGER

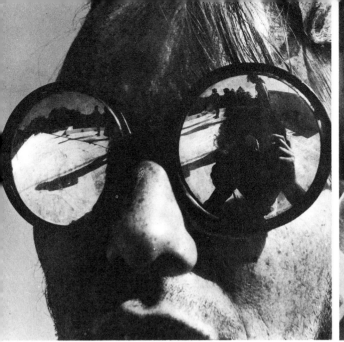

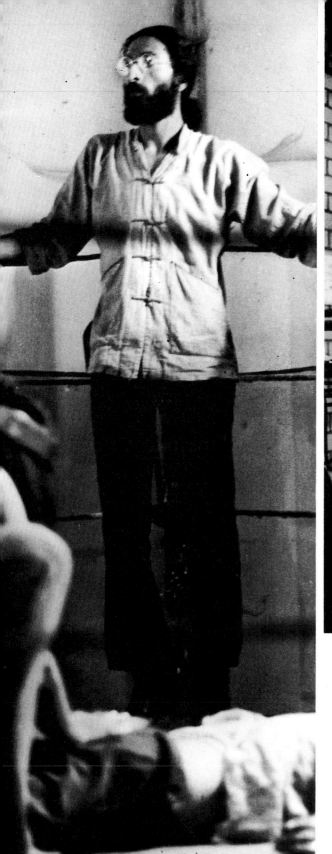

ANTIGONES

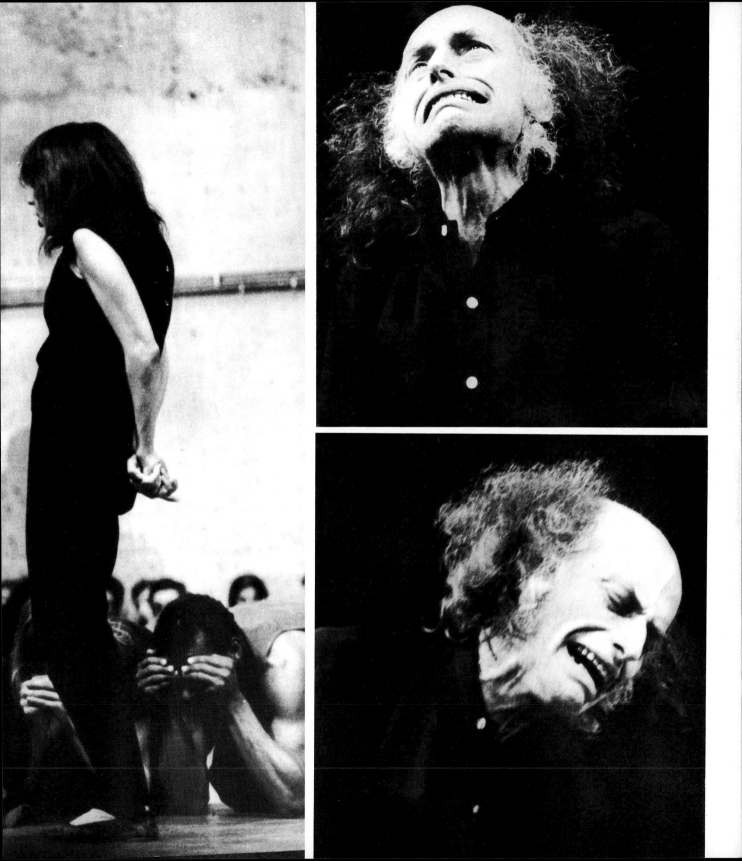

MOROCCO
A DAY

July 19, 1967: Neuilly-sur-Seine. Isha Manna Beck delivered by Dr. Ravina and Beautiful Oriental Midwife at American Hospital of Paris at one thirty PM. Weight: 4 lbs 2oz or 2 Kilos. Visitors: Carl, Julian, Garrick.

July 21, 1967: Neuilly-sur-Seine. All day searching for a name. At sundown (Shabbas) Isha written on a piece of paper from Genesis 2: 23 'She shall be called woman'.

July 22, 1967: Named Isha Manna. Registered at the Mairie de Neuilly by Julian. Isha eats. Nurse reports good progress.

August 4, 1967: Isha comes home to 9 rue Troyon. Her first trip from Neuilly to Paris in the Volkswagen bus driven by Julian is pleasant. She seems to like the bouncing of the bus.

September 6, 1967: Paris. Isha goes to Mme Picard's in the evening when the family plays the Mysteries. Mme Picard introduces Isha to her 8 year old Pascal and her 10 month old son Pierre-Louis and her husband, a Paris taxi driver. Isha sleeps in their dining room under an oil painting of the Bay of Naples.

September 8, 1967: Paris. Isha attends her first post-natal rehearsal. Antigone walk-thru at the Chaptal Theatre. She has excellently behaved, asleep and awake, both when carried in arms thru the stage action or when lying in her straw basket at the end of the middle aisle. She seems not to mind the shouting and the violent action, but watches all peacefully.

September 22, 1967: Paris to Belgrade. In the morning Isha attends an Antigone rehearsal at the Chaptal Theatre. She has never been frightened by the loud sounds of the rehearsal, battle scenes and all; but today, when the actors quarrel and raise their voices for real, she reacts and Odile takes her out of the room. Later she is afraid and starts whenever the actors shout, even in the context of the play. As if the spell were broken. All Isha's things are packed and she leaves the city of her birth to travel to Yugoslavia. A camping-gas stove to sterilize and warm bottles is set up in the narrow Wagon-Lit compartment. 7 bottles of Evian water. Cans of powdered milk, farina, carrots, medication, two thermos bottles, diapers and laundry bags all crowded into the Wagon-Lit. Isha watches the trees go by, watches the sky darken. The shade is pulled. She sleeps thru Italy in her basket at the front of the lower berth. Different countries go by. The conductor collects her passport.

September 24, 1967: Belgrade. Isha stays on a dressing room shelf where Vera Cucnik and the theatre's dressing room attendant watch over her. After the theatre, at dinner, Jerzy Grotowski praises her graceful gestures. She listens attentively but sometimes sleeps as he talks.

September 28, 1967: Paris to Southampton. Isha's first long car ride. She seems to be very happy. She lives in the back seat. Her basket is in the luggage compartment behind mother's seat. She sleeps very peacefully, Julian makes formulas out of two thermos bottles.

September 29, 1967: Southampton to Holy Head. Isha travels on the Oslo to Southampton. Her first time at sea. She goes through customs, she drives across England, stopping at Salisbury Cathedral. Passing thru Tintern Forest and the poetic Abbey, thru Wales, in sunlight and rain, with rainbow to Holyhead.

October 5, 1967: Dublin. Isha attends a press conference at the Hotel Shelbourne where she is much photographed. This rouses the ire of an Irish pressman who feels her presence constitutes cruelty to children. She smiles contentedly however. After the performance Siobhan McKenna comes to talk to the actors and extends her admiration to Isha.

November 1, 1967: Vichy to Bezier. Isha is 5 months old. She travels across the mountains from Vichy to Bezier.

November 2, 1967: Bezier to Barcelona. Isha enters Spain in the beautiful ceremonial robe which Jenny Hecht has made and broidered for her. She arrives in Barcelona on a rainy night. She cries for this is the third long day of travel and it was a very tiring one and it's cold.

November 3, 1967: Barcelona. In the evening she comes to the Teatro Romea and stays backstage during the Antigone performance. A wonderful blackshawled lady watches over her. She is the wife of the theatre's concierge. She does not like Isha to lie in her basket but prefers to wrap her very securely in the Spanish manner, with her face tucked into the end of a peep-hole in the shawl close to her breast. Isha, thus warmly wrapped, sleeps thru the whole performance.

November 9, 1967: Bilbao to St. Sebastian. She drives from Bilbao to St. Sebastian. On a lookout above the Bay of Biscay all the buses of The Living Theatre stop and all the children meet on the high pine cliff. Ali and Isha enjoy a long confrontation. Ali reaches for Isha's hand affectionately. She reaches for his. Chiwe pats her gently on the head. David says 'Isha Isha Isha' pointing at her with delight. Ben smiles and Isha smiles back. All on the cliffs above the Bay of Biscay.

November 24, 1967: Paris. Isha has tea with Salvador Dali. In his salon, at the Hotel Meurice, he receives her with great trepidation. She is dressed in her ceremonial robes and receives the attention of the master calmly. It is he who is excited; 'This is the closest I have ever been to a baby', says the painter 'for they fear me more than they fear lions', and he widens his eyes and looks at her forbiddingly. She remains self-possessed. Dali calls for the photographer and poses with Isha Manna, holding the gold-topped cane of Victor Hugo between their faces. He widens his eyes mysteriously as the camera clicks. He poses her on this side and on that. She keeps her cool. 'It is the walking stick of Hugo'. Gala calls on the telephone. He tells her that there is a small child of 2 years visiting them. Gala arrives and is presented to Isha Manna. The conversation is in French. No one mentions that she is not 2 years old but 4 months old. She is our youngest visitor says Captain Peter Moore, Dali's assistant. Is it a boy or a girl?' says a gorgeous transvestite in English. Isha looks at the moving mirror of a LeParc sculpture, watching the distortions. She is beautiful in the gilt-decorate salon. She too is draped in white and gold. 'Do not go', says Dali until you have met the Prince and the Princess. When the Prince and the Princess arrive, Isha is presented. She is stately and in accordance with courtly manners is graciously bored by her fine surroundings. Dali in purple jacket and striped trousers accompanies her along the long corridor and to the stairway. She returns to the Hotel where she lives, St. Georges Palace, and a garret room that is freezing cold and that won't warm up with the plug-in heaters, where Odile and Gunter watch her during the performance of Antigone.

December 31, 1967: Paris. On the last day of the year of her birth, Isha goes to the Cluny Museum to see the Unicorn Tapestries. She is asleep on arrival, but opens her eyes to see herself surrounded by unicorns. Carl holds her hand to pat the Unicorn's horn that is mounted between the tapestries. Outside it hails and she sits in a Boul' Mich cafe watching the sharp white hail strike the glass wall at nightfall.

January 1, 1968: Paris. She starts the new year happily, proud of her accomplishments, her attempts at standing and sitting up by herself, her sounds, her relationship to her hands and feet and above all, to her growing awareness of her surroundings, her love of all her friends, her reaching out to everyone. Her gestures and actions can be described but the best part is in her gaze filling with knowledge and her looks of recognition and of love. She celebrates Channukah.

January 31, 1968: Rome. Isha is 28 weeks old. She attends a rehearsal. The first discussion of Paradise Now. At Donyale Luna's apartment at 67 Via della Purificazione. Here in a small room are assembled the whole Living Theatre and for the first time all The Living Theatre children. There is Michael Shari, eldest, there are Krystyn and Meegan Shari, there is David Van Tosh, Chiwe Gordon, Ali Noah Antonin Barber, Isha Manna Beck, and Tai Julian Olivier Pannewitz. The first rehearsal proceeded miraculously amid the incredible chaos of the crowded room. The children cause more glee than irritation, but this glee impedes the concentration of the rehearsal.

Febraury 26, 1968: Cefalu. Isha and Krystyn constitute the audience. They sit at one end of the mattress laid out for the children. Michael Shari

mounts Isha's dolls, the white Teddy bear, from Gerard Dechsal, the Paris pacifist, and the glove-doll made by Jenny Hecht, on a pillow which serves as a stage and presents the full puppet version of the Mysteries. 'Look at the people, don't look at the puppet-teer'. Using the two dolls to portray all the characters, he plays out the whole Mysteries from the Brig-Dollar to the Plague. Isha, with Krystyn's arm around her, enjoys the whole spectacle. She is quite aware of the role of spectator. She always responds to actions done in front of her which Julian calls playing theater.

May 16, 1968: Paris. Isha assists in the Occupation of the Odeon Theatre. The stage is occupied by the students' discussions as the theatre has been declared a forum on revolutionary action. Isha is greeted by Jean-Jacques Lebel and friends, and being accus-tomed to playing on stage she occupies herself during the speech-making. She spends some time in the office of Jean-Louis Barrault where Madeleine Renaud especially admires her. tho they are too preoccupied and she is too sleepy for them to appreciate each-other properly. Barrault is about to resign as the Director of the Theatre de France, and Isha is cranky because her bottle is finished. But they are both polite and she says hello and he smiles.

May 17, 1968: Paris. She leaves Paris amidst news of growing strikes and occupations.

May 18, 1968: Avignon. Arriving in Avignon to select rooms for the next two months, the build-ing is an old school called the Vieille Ecole Frederic Mistral. The previous residents were the CRS, the riot-control division of the po-lice. The rooms still bear traces of their occupancy. The door to Isha's room is heavy metal with a small square of glass at eye-level. The windows are bar-red with heavy prison bars. There is a company meeting but Isha is too restless and is taken for a walk in the night streets of Avi-gnon.

May 24, 1968: Avignon. She says, 'Tai, David, Dollie, Hello, Cookie'.

July 19, 1968: Avignon. Isha Man-na's first birthday. When she woke there was a birthday table all set up with paper flowers and bouquets made of the drawings of the Beaux-Arts students. Julian decorated the desk-top with boats and flowers and forms and presents from friends and mem-bers of the company. She ap-preciates that it is a special day. But what is the world like in her first year? She is above all gen-tle. She has a winning softness that is amazing to all. Yet she is the most active of children. She is totally out-going, recogniz-ing everyone's presences and demanding love from them. Nor does she hesitate to give affec-tion. She bestows kisses readily and often and to many people. Her trust in love is unqualified. She makes no conditions. For everyone she has a special ra-diance. Responding to each ac-cording to what is given her and adding to each her love. She is discovering the world, con-structing a conscious image of

eality. And at each new aspect of the world that presents itself, at each new discovery, she expresses delight. Delight that it should be so s it is. And everyone who is with her experiences this delight and this discovery with her, and this way she leads everyone to the secret garden. uly 20, 1968: Avignon. All day there are rumors of tension in the city. There are people in Avignon who do not like The Living Theatre and they ave been urged to attack. The atmosphere is tense. Isha hears everyone talking a lot in a strained voice. In the afternoon she comes to the theatre • watch the rehearsal of a new end for Antigone with the company of the Chien Noir whose play has been prohibited. During the performance dile brings Tai down to Isha's room to look after both of them together. After the theatre they are, all three of them, asleep under the mosquito etting. Mother and Carl go out for a café. Julian stayed in the room to talk ... to Saul Gottlieb. There is a threatening incident with some shouting oys on the street, so that mother and Carl return quickly to find Isha awake and a scene of great dismay in the room. This is what had happened. s Isha and Tai and Odile lay sleeping, Julian heard a shouting group coming down the street. About 20 people quickly ran into the room for protec- on and shut the large metal door, against the invaders. They began to pound on the door with a battering-ram, a 4x4 with jagged ends. Saul and ulian tried to push the desk in front of the door. After several jabs at the door the missile shattered the small cell-window in the door. The object pped thru the map of the North Pole which covered the window in the door. If flew (with what force it must have been hurled) into the room, d struck Saul Gottlieb on the nose, injuring him. Isha woke. Whether it was the shattering of the glass or the tearing of the paper map, or the xclamation of horror by the people in the room at the sight of this weapon flying thru the door is not certain. She cried. Odile woke and went to the eeping Tai and Mary Mary ran to pick up Isha as Julian shouted in French, 'There are children in here, there are tiny children in here'. Whether response to the presence of the children or whether they had done their mischief in penetrating the door, the attackers left. The doors to the street ere bolted. Already there were other hostile groups at the other doors. Isha cried a few minutes at the sudden awakening, then was cheerful and rateful to find herself in a room full of people all talking in excited tones and all that tension and energy in the room. Glass and blood on the floor. he windows of the room give on to the street and they are barred because this place was a prison for the CRS, they are not safe for her. Isha moves pstairs to Luke's large room on the 2nd story where there is a large flight of stairs between the attackers below and her mosquito-net covered bed. ll the other entrances are attacked. The rooms are kept dark as a precaution. All night from the courtyard sounds of metal pipes striking the doors, reaking glass, and shouting. But Isha sleeps. All that Isha knows is that she woke with a start, that there were excited people talking, that she ayed for a while and went to sleep in another room. Is that all that she knows?

Now we have to speak in self tones in
rehearsal --
Now we must give up drugs /
Treason + rot exists

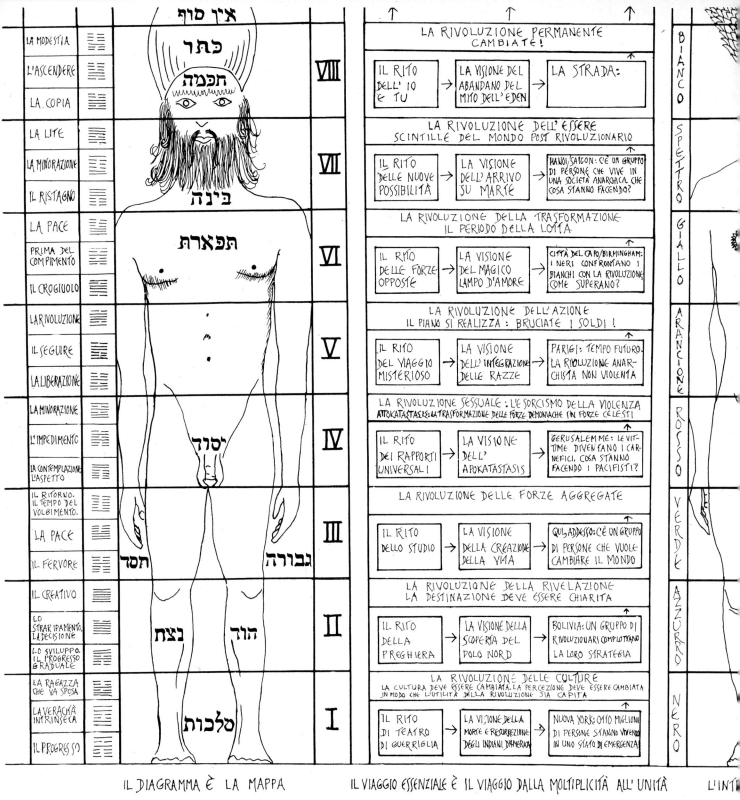

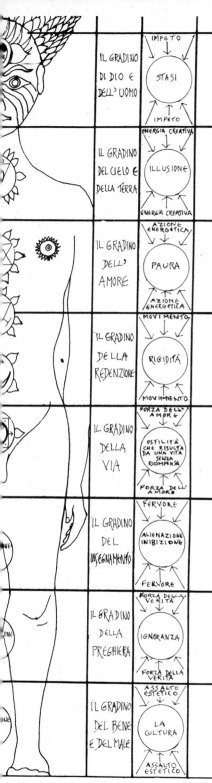

IL GRADINO DI DIO E DELL'UOMO	IMPETO → STASI ← IMPETO	
IL GRADINO DEL CIELO E DELLA TERRA	ENERGIA CREATIVA → ILLUSIONE ← ENERGIA CREATIVA	
IL GRADINO DELL'AMORE	AZIONE ENERGETICA → PAURA ← AZIONE ENERGETICA	
IL GRADINO DELLA REDENZIONE	MOVIMENTO → RIGIDITÀ ← MOVIMENTO	
IL GRADINO DELLA VIA	FORZA DELL'AMORE → OSTILITÀ CHE RISULTA DA UNA VITA SENZA RICOMPENSA ← FORZA DELL'AMORE	
IL GRADINO DEL INSEGNAMENTO	FERVORE → ALIENAZIONE INIBIZIONE ← FERVORE	
IL GRADINO DELLA PREGHIERA	FORZA DELLA VERITÀ → IGNORANZA ← FORZA DELLA VERITÀ	
IL GRADINO DEL BENE E DEL MALE	ASSALTO ESTETICO → LA CULTURA ← ASSALTO ESTETICO	

RIVOLUZIONE
OLLETTIVA

PARADISE NOW

COME OUT TO PLAY BOYS AND GIRLS

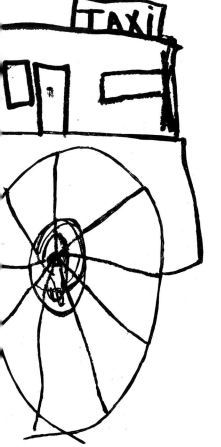

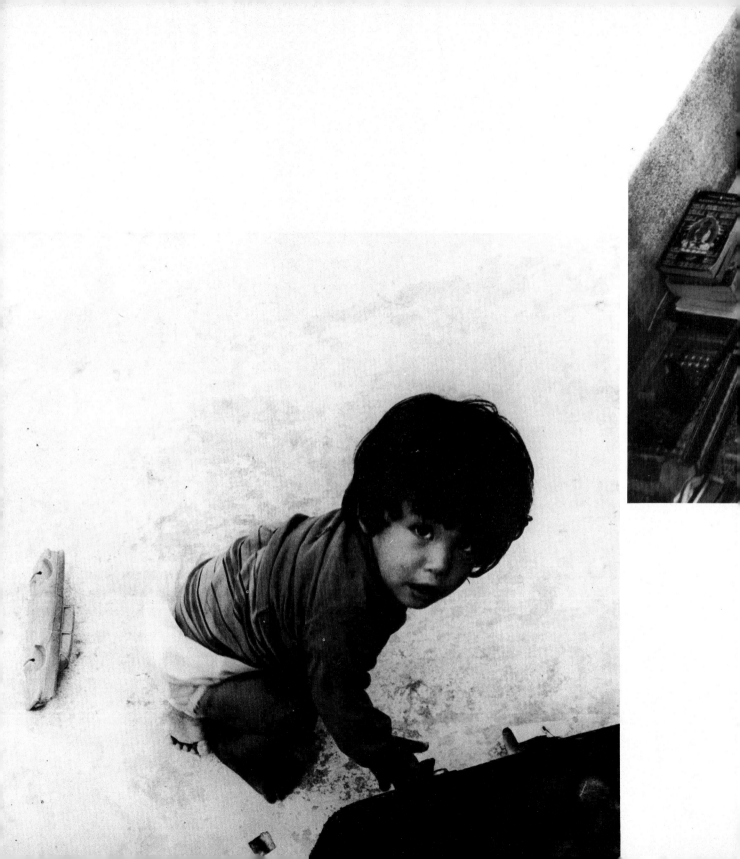

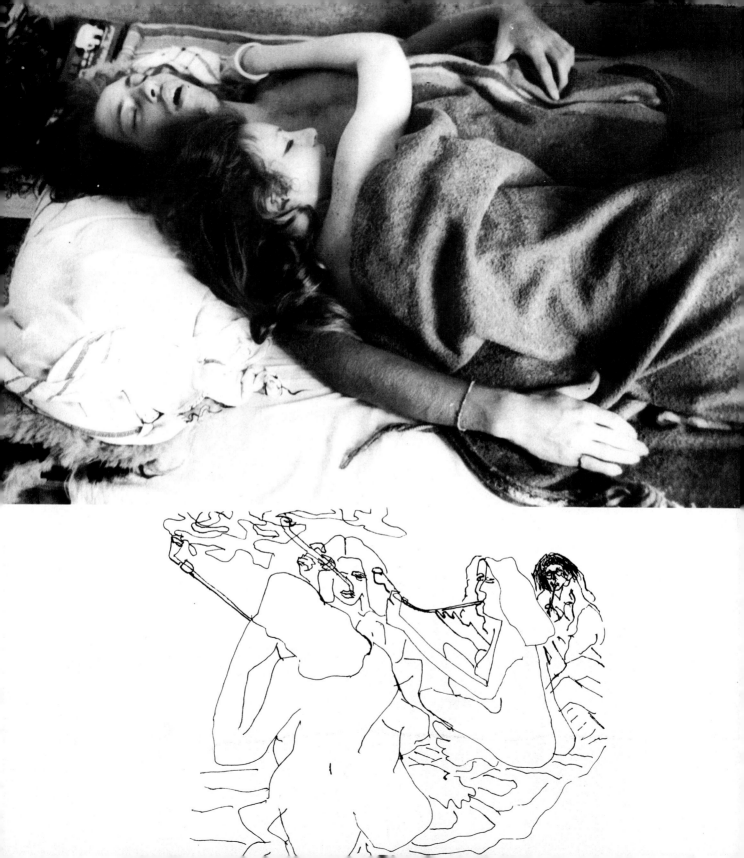

LIVING THEATRE ACTION LAST DECLARATION

The structure is crumbling. All of the institutions are feeling the tremors. How do you respond to the emergency?

For the sake of mobility The Living Theatre is dividing into four cells. One cell is currently located in Paris and the center of its orientation is chiefly political. Another is located in Berlin and its orientation is cultural. A fourth is on its way to India and its orientation is spiritual. If the structure is to be transformed it has to be attacked from many sides. This is what we are seeking to do.

In the world today there are many movements seeking to transform this structure ... the Capitalist - Bureaucratic - Military - Authoritarian - Police Complex ... into its opposite: a Non-Violent-Communal-Organism. The structure will fall if it's pushed the right way. Our purpose is to lend our support to all the forces of liberation.

But first we have to get out of the trap. Buildings called theaters are an architectural trap. The man in the street will never enter such a building.

1. Because he can't: the theater buildings belong to those who can afford to get in; all buildings are property held by the Establishment by force of arms.
2. Because the life he leads at work and out of work exhausts him.
3. Because inside they speak in a code of things which are neither interesting to him nor in his interest.

The Living Theatre doesn't want to perform for the privileged elite anymore because all privilege is violence to the underprivileged.

Therefore The Living Theatre doesn't want to perform in theater buildings anymore. Get out of the trap; the structure is crumbling.

The Living Theatre doesn't want to be an institution anymore. It is out front clear that all institutions are rigid and support the Establishment. After 20 years the structure of The Living Theatre had become institutionalized. All the institutions are crumbling. The Living Theatre had to crumble or change its form.

How do you get out of the trap?

1. Liberate yourself as much as possible from dependence on the established economic system. It was not easy for The Living Theatre to divide its community, because the community was living and working together in love. Not dissension, but revolutionary needs had divided us. A small group can survive with cunning and daring. It is now for each cell to find means of surviving without becoming a consumer product.
2. Abandon the theatres. Create other circumstances for theater for the man in the street. Create circumstances that will lead to Action which is the highest form of theater we know. Create Action.
3. Find new forms. Smash the art barrier. Art is confined in the jail of the Establishment's mentality. That's how art is made to function to serve the needs of the Upper Classes. If art can't be used to serve the needs of the people, get rid of it. We only need art if it can be the truth so that it can become clear to everyone what has to be done and how to do it.